MY FIRST SPANISH PICTURE DICTIONARY

Mi primer diccionario de imágenes español-inglés

Dalmatian 🐾 Press

15423 My First Spanish Picture Dictionary
ISBN: 1-40372-561-6
06 07 08 WAI 10 9 8 7 6 5 4 3 2 1

Note to parents

My First Spanish Picture Dictionary provides a wonderful way to introduce children to the world of language. By helping your child repeat the simple text next to each photograph, you can encourage essential literacy skills. Your child will delight in familiar objects and discover new favorites. By making learning language fun and exciting, **My First Spanish Picture Dictionary** encourages vital vocabulary building in young learners.

Nota a los padres

Mi primer diccionario de imágenes español-inglés proporciona un maravilloso camino para introducir a los niños en el mundo del idioma. Al ayudar a sus niños a repetir el texto simple junto a cada fotografía, pueden fomentar habilidades esenciales de alfabetización. Sus niños se deleitarán con objetos conocidos y descubrirán nuevos objetos favoritos. Al hacer que el aprendizaje del idioma sea entretenido y emocionante, **Mi primer diccionario de imágenes español-inglés** fomenta el desarrollo del vocabulario vital en los estudiantes jóvenes.

Table of Contents   Índice de materia

La guía de pronunciación
Pronunciation guide

How to pronounce the names of the letters in Spanish:

Aa ...... ah	**Jj** .... hótah	**Rr** .... éreh
Bb ...... beh	**Kk** ...... kah	**Ss** .... éseh
Cc .... seh	**Ll** .... éleh	**Tt** .... teh
Ch ch .. cheh	**Ll ll** ...... éyeh	**Uu** ...... oo
Dd ...... deh	**Mm** .... émeh	**Vv** ...... beh
Ee .... eh	**Nn** ...... éneh	**Ww** .... dóbleh beh
Ff .... éfeh	**Ññ** ...... ényeh	**Xx** ...... ékees
Gg ...... heh	**Oo** ...... oh	**Yy** ...... ee gree éh gah
Hh ...... ácheh	**Pp** ...... peh	**Zz** ...... sehtah
Ii .... ee	**Qq** ...... koo	

How to pronounce the vowels in Spanish:

A pronounced as "ah" as in father   much**a**s, gr**a**ci**a**s, **a**nim**a**les

E pronounced as a short "eh" as in men and ten   com**e**, di**e**z

I pronounced as "ee" as in knee and bee   r**í**o, **i**nsecto

O pronounced as a long "o" as in go   r**o**j**o**, c**o**nej**o**

U pronounced as "oo" as in "pool"   **u**vas, J**u**an

How to pronounce the consonants in Spanish:

Most of the consonants in Spanish sound very similar to those in English. However, there are a few that are Spanish specific:

b/v	"b" and "v" sound the same in Spanish. They are pronounced with a sound that is close to the English "b" with a slight hint of the English "v" sound.	**v**aca, **v**entana
c	"c" sounds like the "c" in car. When "c" is followed by an "i" or an "e," it sounds like "s."	**c**aimán, **c**in**c**o, **c**ir**c**o
h	"h" is silent in Spanish, except after "c."	**h**ogar, **h**oja, **h**elado, co**h**ete
j	"j" sounds like a stronger version of the English letter "h."	**j**ugo, **j**uego, cone**j**o
ll	"Ll" sounds like the "y" in "yellow."	amari**ll**o, **ll**uvia
ñ	The tilde mark (~) above the "n" makes the "n" sound like the "ni" in "onion."	oto**ñ**o, monta**ñ**a
qu	"q" and "u" next to each other sound like the "k" in "kind."	**qu**iero, **qu**eso
r	In Spanish, the "r" is rolled, making a trilling sound in the following instances: 1) at the beginning of a word. 2) when it's double in the middle of a word. 3) after "l" or "n" in the middle of a word.	**r**ápido, a**rr**iba, al**r**ededor, En**r**ique
y	"y" sounds like the "y" in yellow. When "y" is alone or at the end of a word, it is pronounced like the "ee" in feet.	**Y**olanda, **y**
z	"z" sounds like "s."	**z**anahoria, **z**orro

Lo que hacemos
Things we do

sonreír
smile

abrazar
hug

besar
kiss

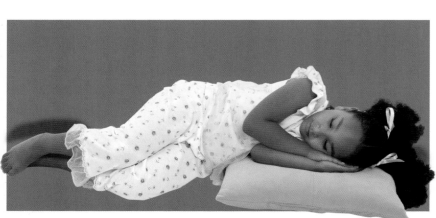

dormir
sleep

gritar
shout

jugar
play

inclinarse
bend

estirarse
stretch

saltar
jump

la parada de manos
handstand

Hacer música
Making music

las panderetas
tambourines

la flauta
recorder

el violín
violín

los cascabeles
jingle bells

el xilófono
xylophone

la trompeta
trumpet

las maracas
maracas

la guitarra
guitar

el acordeón
accordion

la familia
family

los abuelos
grandparents

La familia
Family

el hijo
son

el papá
father

las hermanas
sisters

la mamá
mother

la hija
daughter

los hermanos
brothers

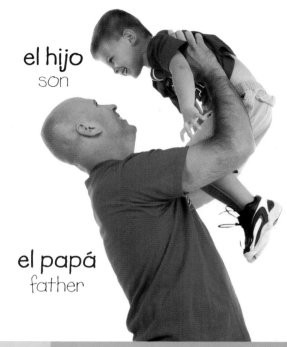

Mi ropa
My clothes

los pantalones cortos
shorts

el paraguas
umbrella

las botas
boots

el abrigo
coat

el impermeable
rain jacket

los pantalones
pants

el suéter
sweater

la camiseta
t-shirt

los calcetines
socks

los mitones
mittens

los zapatos
shoes

las zapatillas
sneakers

el gorro
winter hat

la pijama
pajamas

el vestido
dress

la chaqueta
jacket

11

Las mascotas
Pets

el perro
dog

los cachorros
puppies

el hueso
bone

los gatitos
kittens

el pez de colores
goldfish

la lagartija
lizard

la cucha del perro
dog house

el gato cat

el ratón mouse

el loro parrot

la tortuga turtle

el conejo rabbit

el hámster hamster

el cobayo guinea pig

13

En el baño
In the bathroom

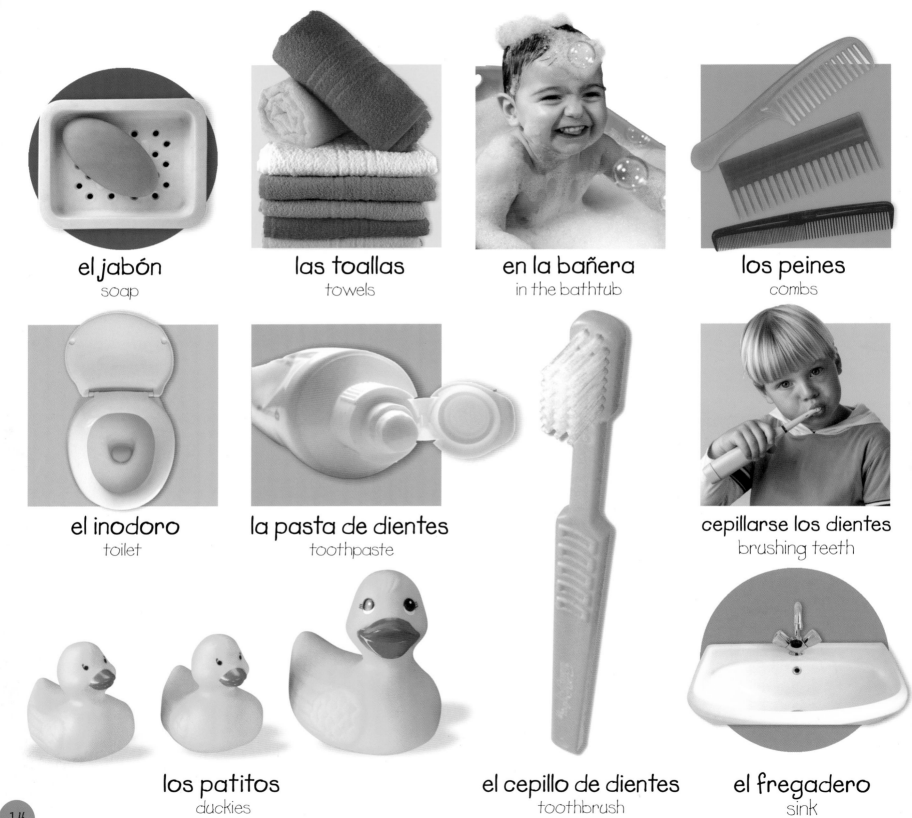

el jabón
soap

las toallas
towels

en la bañera
in the bathtub

los peines
combs

el inodoro
toilet

la pasta de dientes
toothpaste

cepillarse los dientes
brushing teeth

los patitos
duckies

el cepillo de dientes
toothbrush

el fregadero
sink

el teléfono
telephone

el sofá
sofa

la alcancía
piggy bank

la televisión
television

la silla
chair

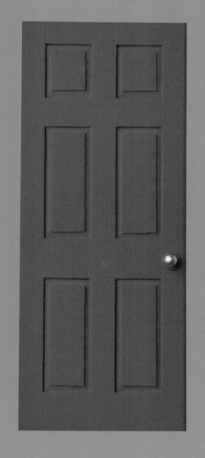

el reloj
clock

la casa
house

la puerta
door

15

Las frutas y verduras
Fruits and vegetables

la naranja
orange

el kiwi
kiwi

la banana
banana

la manzana
apple

las cerezas
cherries

la piña
pineapple

la fresa
strawberry

las uvas
grapes

el melón
melon

16

las arvejas
peas

los champiñones
mushrooms

la berenjena
eggplant

los pimientos
peppers

la cebolla
onion

la calabaza
pumpkin

la coliflor
cauliflower

los espárragos
asparagus

los tomates
tomatoes

17

En la playa
At the beach

la cometa
kite

los cocos
coconuts

la gaviota
seagull

el sombrero
hat

las conchas
seashells

las ojotas
flip-flops

el traje de baño
swimsuit

el flotador
float

hacer esnórquel
to snorkel

el cangrejo
crab

el balón
ball

los anteojos de sol
sunglasses

jugando en la arena
playing in the sand

el balde
pail

la sombrilla
parasol

19

En el bosque
In the woods

la serpiente
snake

la hoja
leaf

la mariposa
butterfly

el cervatillo
fawn

el águila
eagle

el mapache
raccoon

la ardilla
squirrel

la hormiga
ant

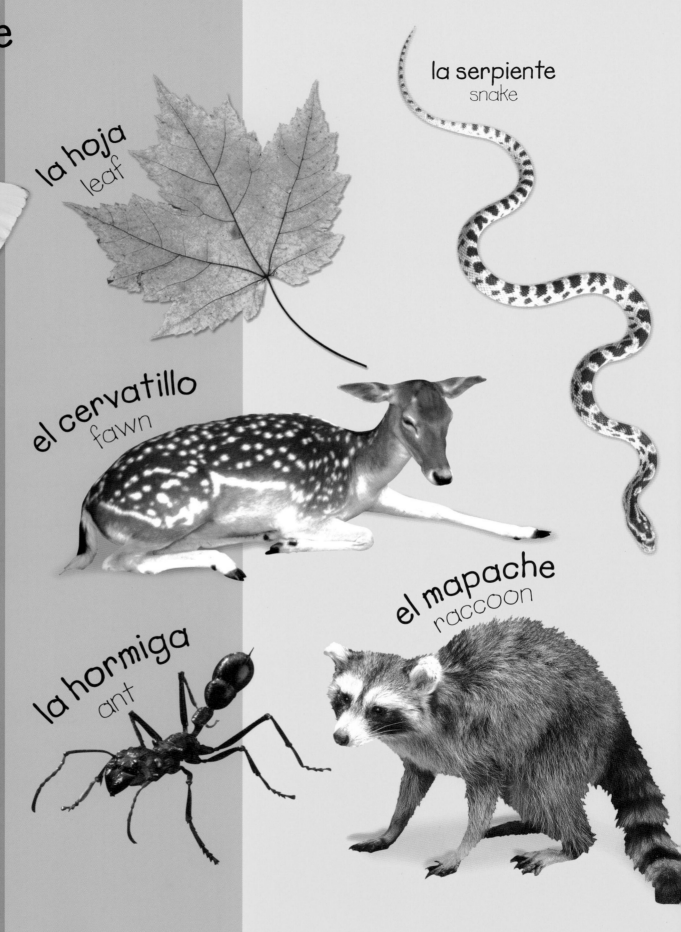

la mariquita
ladybug

la bellota
acorn

el pájaro
bird

el búho
owl

el nido
nest

la araña
spider

la rana
frog

el zorro
fox

Mi comida favorita
My favorite food

el pastelito
cupcake

la tarta
pie

la leche
milk

el jugo de naranja
orange juice

el pavo
turkey

los huevos
eggs

las galletas
cookies

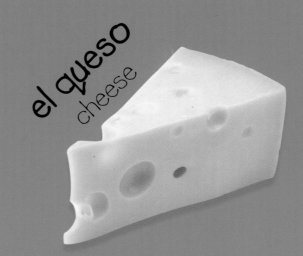

el queso
cheese

22

los espaguetis
spaghetti

el pollo
chicken

la hamburguesa
hamburger

el helado
ice cream

el sándwich
sandwich

las patatas fritas
french fries

la pizza
pizza

el pan
bread

la miel
honey

La escuela
School

la niña
girl

el niño
boy

la maestra
teacher

las tijeras
scissors

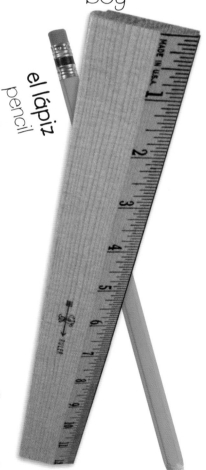

el lápiz
pencil

la regla
ruler

el globo terráqueo
globe

la goma de borrar
eraser

los crayones
crayons

el pegamento
glue

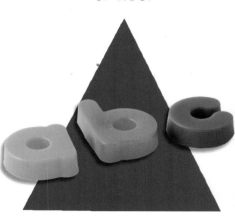

las letras
letters

los proyectos de arte
art projects

el autobús escolar
school bus

los alumnos
students

leer
to read

la computadora
computer

pintar
to paint

El parque de diversiones
Amusement park

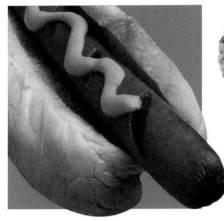

el perrito caliente
hot dog

las manzanas con caramelo
caramel apples

el carrusel
carousel

las palomitas de maíz
popcorn

la rueda
ferris wheel

el payaso
clown

los dulces
candies

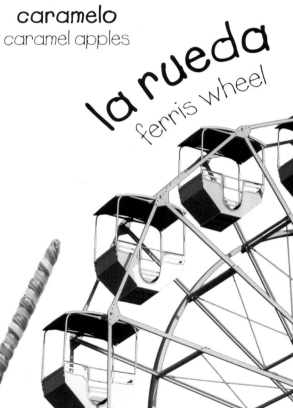

La fiesta de cumpleaños
Birthday party

el pastel
cake

los regalos
gifts

los globos
balloons

las velitas
candles

el helado
ice cream

el moño
bow

los sombreros de fiesta
party hats

las piruletas
lollipops

la piñata
piñata

Los juguetes
Toys

el molinete
pinwheel

el carrito
wagon

el carro
car

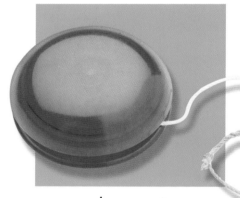

el yoyó
yo-yo

el volquete
dump truck

las canicas
marbles

las pompas
bubbles

el triciclo
tricycle

la muñeca
doll

el osito de peluche
teddy bear

la varita mágica
magic wand

los bloques
blocks

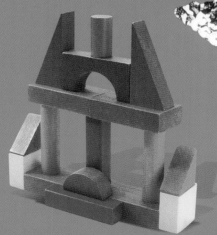

el dinosaurio
dinosaur

el tren
train

las acuarelas
paints

29

Los deportes
Sports

el tenis
tennis

el béisbol
baseball

el baloncesto
basketball

andar
en bicicleta
to ride a bike

los bolos
bowling

el fútbol
americano
football

esquiar
skiing

el hockey
hockey

los patines de hielo
ice skates

la animadora
cheerleader

el karate
karate

el boxeo
boxing

31

En el mar
In the ocean

el pez
fish

bucear
scuba diving

el delfín
dolphin

el pingüino
penguin

la tortuga de mar
sea turtle

el tiburón
shark

la langosta
lobster

el pulpo
octopus

el velero
sailboat

la ola
wave

la foca
seal

la estrella de mar
starfish

33

La zona de construcción
Construction zone

la excavadora
digger

el martillo
hammer

el casco
helmet

los clavos
nails

la carretilla
wheelbarrow

los guantes
gloves

el serrucho
handsaw

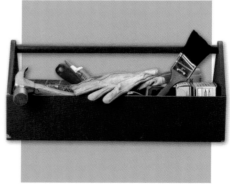

la caja de herramientas
toolbox

la escalera
ladder

las señales de tránsito
traffic signs

el cono
cone

Las profesiones
Professions

el doctor
doctor

el constructor
builder

la artista
artist

el cocinero
chef

la enfermera
nurse

el policía
police officer

Los animales salvajes
Wild animals

el cocodrilo
crocodile

el elefante
elephant

el gorila
gorilla

el tigre
tiger

el león
lion

la iguana
iguana

el tucán
toucan

la jirafa
giraffe

el koala
koala

el pavo real
peacock

la cebra
zebra

el oso
bear

el oso polar
polar bear

Los medios de transporte
Transportation vehicles

la motocicleta
motorcycle

el camión
truck

el camión de bomberos
fire truck

las llantas
tires

la ambulancia
ambulance

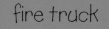

las llaves
keys

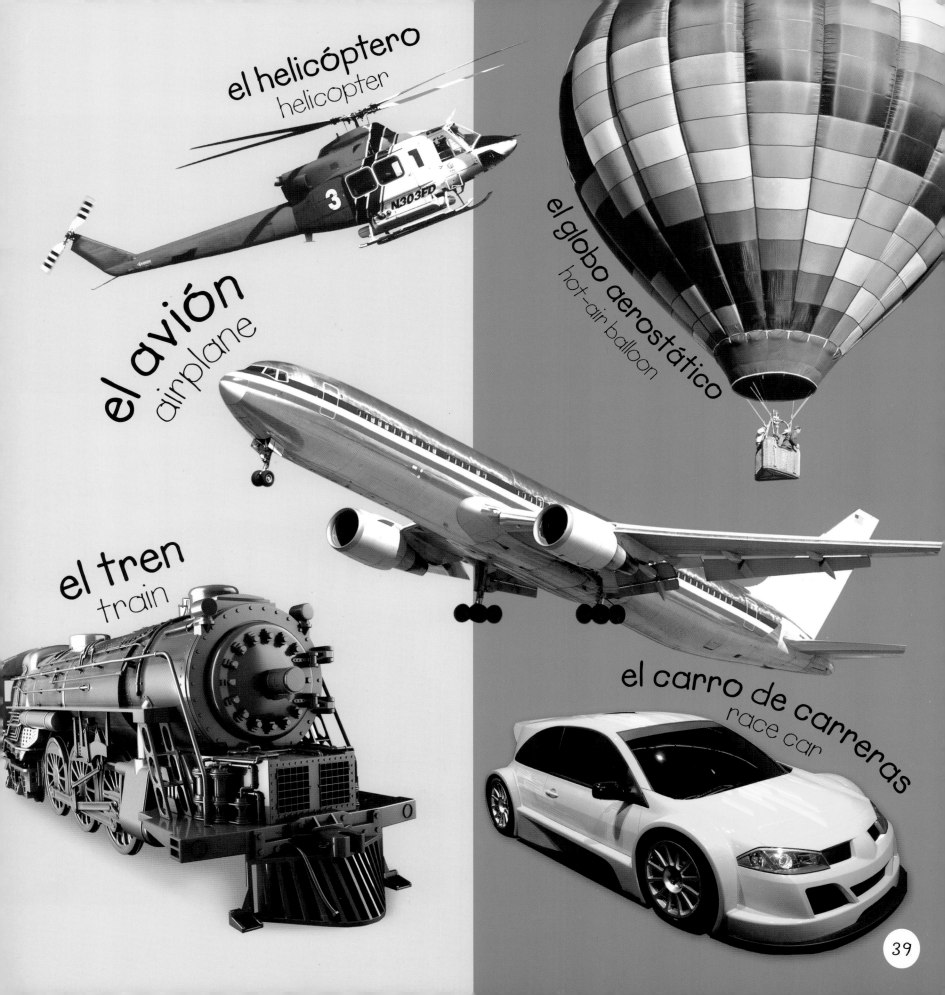

el helicóptero
helicopter

el globo aerostático
hot-air balloon

el avión
airplane

el tren
train

el carro de carreras
race car

39

En la granja
On the farm

el granero
barn

el maíz
corn

el espantapájaros
scarecrow

el girasol
sunflower

el tractor
tractor

la valla
fence

la paja
hay

la cabra
goat

el cerdo
pig

el pavo
turkey

la vaca
cow

la llama
llama

el caballo
horse

los pollitos
chicks

la oveja
sheep

41

Los colores
Colors

rojo red

naranja orange

amarillo yellow

verde green

azul blue

morado purple

rosa pink

blanco white

marrón brown

negro black

Las formas
Shapes

el círculo
circle

el triángulo
triangle

el cuadrado
square

la estrella
star

el rombo
diamond

el rectángulo
rectangle

el óvalo
oval

la media luna
crescent

el hexágono
hexagon

el corazón
heart

Los números

Numbers

0 cero
zero

1 uno
one

2 dos
two

3 tres
three

8 ocho
eight

9 nueve
nine

10 diez
ten

11 once
eleven

15 quince
fifteen

16 dieciséis
sixteen

17 diecisiete
seventeen

4

cuatro
four

5

cinco
five

6

seis
six

7

siete
seven

12

doce
twelve

13

trece
thirteen

14

catorce
fourteen

18

dieciocho
eighteen

19

diecinueve
nineteen

20

veinte
twenty

Los días de la semana
Days of the week

Lunes	Martes	Miércoles	Jue
Monday	Tuesday	Wednesday	Thu

Los meses del año
Months of the year

Enero	Febrero
January	February
Mayo	**Junio**
May	June
Septiembre	**Octubre**
September	October

| ...es | Viernes | Sábado | Domingo |
| ...day | Friday | Saturday | Sunday |

Marzo
March

Abril
April

Julio
July

Agosto
August

Noviembre
November

Diciembre
December

47